Understanding Personality

Toney Allman

San Diego, CA

© 2018 ReferencePoint Press, Inc.
Printed in the United States

For more information, contact:
ReferencePoint Press, Inc.
PO Box 27779
San Diego, CA 92198
www. ReferencePointPress.com

LIBRARY OF CONGRESS CATALOGING-IN-PUBLICATION DATA

Name: Allman, Toney, author.
Title: Understanding Personality/by Toney Allman.
Description: San Diego, CA: ReferencePoint Press, [2018] | Series:
   Understanding Psychology | Includes bibliographical references and index.
Identifiers: LCCN 2016046633 (print) | LCCN 2017003008 (ebook) | ISBN
   9781682822777 (hardback) | ISBN 9781682822784 (eBook)
Subjects: LCSH: Personality—Juvenile literature.
Classification: LCC BF698 .A378 2018 (print) | LCC BF698 (ebook) | DDC
   155.2--dc23
LC record available at https://lccn.loc.gov/2016046633

CONTENTS

The Human Brain: Thought, Behavior, and Emotion

Frontal lobe controls:
- Thinking
- Planning
- Organizing
- Problem solving
- Short-term memory
- Movement
- Personality
- Emotions
- Behavior
- Language

Parietal lobe:
- Interprets sensory information, such as taste, temperature, and touch

Temporal lobe:
- Processes information from the senses of smell, taste, and sound
- Plays role in memory storage

Occipital lobe:
- Processes images from the eyes
- Links information with images stored in memory

Source: Mayo Foundation for Education and Research, "Slide Show: How Your Brain Works." www.mayoclinic.org.

What Is Personality?

Defining *personality* is difficult. Even among psychologists, psychiatrists, and personality researchers, there is disagreement about what personality is. Yet almost everyone has an idea about what is meant by *personality*. For instance, a student might say, "That is so like Mom. She is always worrying about what could go wrong," or "My friend Joe has such a quick temper. No wonder he rages at other drivers when they cut him off." People recognize that everyone seems to have a character or nature that is abiding and in many ways unique. Personality is the qualities, behaviors, emotions, and actions that make an individual different from other people.

Experts, however, strive to define *personality* in a way that can be agreed on by most people in their field and is measurable and scientific. A generally accepted definition is put forth by the American Psychological Association, which says, "Personality refers to individual differences in characteristic patterns of thinking, feeling and behaving. The study of personality focuses on two broad areas: One is understanding individual differences in particular personality characteristics, such as sociability or irritability. The other is understanding how the various parts of a person come together as a whole."[1] Patterns are customary behaviors or ways of thinking that remain somewhat permanent and stable over time. The patterns for each individual are the characteristics that make the person's personality unique. This does not mean that a person's response in a single situation is predictable; no one responds the same way to every situation all the time. It means that in general a person is more likely than not to respond in certain ways. For example, the individual who is characteristically sociable may, on one evening, choose to stay home alone rather than go out with friends. But in general, over many evenings, that person will probably choose going out with friends and socializing more often than not. Sociability is just a part of that person's nature. For every person, the varying patterns of behavior fit together to make a whole, individual personality. Each personality is different, despite the characteristics that people share in common with one another.

Toward a Theory of Personality

Throughout the history of psychology, researchers and doctors have struggled to understand and define human nature and to explain individual differences. Many of these psychologists have put forth different theories about what personality is and how it determines an individual's patterns of behavior. Different psychological researchers emphasized different aspects of personality. Sigmund Freud, the founder of modern psychiatry, stressed learning to control inborn instincts, such as aggressiveness, selfishness, and pleasure seeking. Others emphasized different basic dimensions of human nature, such as feelings of inferiority versus finding self-worth or the innate human need for socialization and positive relationships with others. Gordon W. Allport, who lived from 1897 to 1967, was one of the first psychologists to theorize about and study personality in terms of specific traits that could be measured and observed by psychologists. He saw traits such as enthusiasm, friendliness, ambitiousness, and dominance as the dimensions that make up each personality. He actually ended up naming some eighteen thousand different traits.

WORDS IN CONTEXT
trait
A distinguishing characteristic or quality.

The trouble with all these personality theories was that each seemed to concentrate on different aspects of personality, and nothing seemed to connect or come together to form a coherent whole. Then during the 1970s, Paul T. Costa Jr. and Robert R. McCrae of the National Institutes of Health, Warren Norman of the University of Michigan, and Lewis Goldberg of the University of

Oregon made a discovery. Through a complicated mathematical and statistical procedure called factor analysis, they determined that all the traits, patterns, and dimensions studied by different theorists did connect with each other. All the traits that others were studying could be statistically determined to fall under the umbrella of just five personality dimensions. The traits could all be reduced to and subsumed in these five dimensions of personality. Costa and McCrae say that these five factors are "the Christmas tree on which . . . [all the other traits] are hung like ornaments."[2]

The Big Five

Today this five-factor model of personality is accepted by most psychologists and psychological researchers as the way to understand, describe, and study personality. The model, commonly

Sigmund Freud (pictured in 1938) founded modern psychiatry. Freud's theories of personality included an emphasis on learning to control inborn instincts, such as aggressiveness, selfishness, and pleasure seeking.

WORDS IN CONTEXT

continuum
A continuous range or sequence with distinct extremes.

called the big five, is used to explain what character is, how individual human nature varies, and how people make choices in their lives. The general consensus is that the five factors are broad traits that exist in all people in varying degrees. Each factor, or trait, can be thought of as a continuum, with people being anywhere on the continuum from very high to very low and at all points in between.

The five factors are:

- **Extraversion:** High levels represent enthusiasm, sociability, and emotional expressiveness. Low levels represent a tendency toward quietness, coolness, and aloofness.

- **Agreeableness:** High levels represent friendliness, empathy, and a trusting approach to life. Low levels represent hostility and unfriendliness.

- **Neuroticism:** High levels represent high stress and a tendency to worry. Low levels represent emotional calmness and stability.

- **Conscientiousness**: High levels represent being organized and dutiful in terms of work and goals. Low levels represent spontaneity and carelessness.

- **Openness:** High levels represent creativity, imaginativeness, and interest in new ideas. Low levels represent practicality, conventional thinking, and preferences for the traditional.

Where an individual falls on the continuum of each of the five factors represents his or her own personality. No person is all one way or another; each individual is just higher or lower on the continuum. Where one person falls on the continuum for each of these five factors cannot be characterized as right or wrong or more or less valuable than where another person might appear.

Why Define *Personality*?

Researchers and psychologists view the five-factor model as a very useful way to describe personality. However, in many ways — at least until actual human brains can be mapped to demonstrate the existence of each factor — personality and individual differences in personality continue to be the subjects of research rather than certainties. The goal of all this research is to understand, describe, and explain personality in order to be able to predict behavior and reactions and ultimately to help individuals understand and be in control of their behavior patterns and improve the quality of their lives.

CHAPTER 1

How Does Personality Develop?

Infants are already distinct individuals when they are born, even though a complete personality has not yet formed. They have different temperaments. Temperaments are the inborn traits that determine how a baby will interact with the world. Most researchers agree that many of the determinants of personality (including temperament) are inborn, or genetically set. Then, as temperament interacts with experience, a personality gradually forms. Generally, by about the first grade, the child's personality is set for life. Psychologists theorize that 50 percent of personality is determined by genes and 50 percent by the environment.

Temperament

Every parent knows that even babies in the same family can be very different from one another. Some newborns are fussy, while others are relatively calm and happy. Some babies are irritable, while others do not react strongly to loud noises or sudden movements. Some seem to be active, while others are cuddlers. As babies, pediatrician Robert Needlman explains, "one child is bubbly and outgoing; another is quiet and observant. One child seems to respond to any small change in temperature, noise, or light level; another barely seems to notice. One child always starts with a positive outlook; another starts with the negative and has to be won over to the positive."[3]

Psychologists have identified nine temperament traits that seem to exist from birth. The first is activity level, which can range from preferring to sit and watch what is happening to being high energy, wiggly, and always on the go. Next is distractibility, a measure of concentration and attention. Some children can concentrate on a task and tune out what is going on in the environment, while others constantly switch their attention from one event to another. Intensity is the energy with which a child responds to any emotion. Highly intense children may experience great depths of emotion, such as delight or despair. Regularity refers to how predictable or unpredictable a child's inborn patterns are. For instance, the child may sleep and eat at certain regular times each day or vary in hunger and tiredness at times that parents cannot predict. Sensory threshold is defined as how sensitive the child's five senses are. One infant may startle dramatically, for example, to a sudden sound in the house (hearing), while another barely notices and sleeps right through it. Highly sensitive children may also react badly to itchy clothing (touch) or become picky eaters (taste).

Another basic temperament trait is labeled approach/withdrawal. It is a measure of how easily a child accepts new situations or people. Some infants are slow to accept new people and hesitant in any strange situation. Others eagerly approach and reach out for new experiences. The trait of adaptability is similar to approach/withdrawal. Some infants and young children easily accept changes and can move from one activity to the next without distress. Others are slow to adapt to change and dislike being rushed from one activity to another. Persistence is another trait in which children can vary dramatically. At one extreme is the child who is stubborn in the face of an obstacle and cannot stop trying to overcome it (whether it is a toy puzzle to solve or a parent who will not give the child a cookie). At the other extreme is the child who easily interrupts a difficult activity and moves on to something else (often cooperating with a parent's decision). The final temperament trait is mood. Mood is basically the trait that determines how positively or negatively the child sees the world. It refers to how generally upbeat or serious the child is. The Child Development Institute explains mood by asking, "Does the child see the glass as half full? Does he focus on the positive aspects of life? Is the child generally in a happy mood? Or, does the child see the glass as half empty and tend to focus on the negative aspects of life?"[4]

None of these temperament traits is bad or good. Each has both positive and negative value, depending on the situation. Highly intense children may be difficult for parents to handle, for instance, but they may grow up to be talented and creative in artistic endeavors. Children who see the glass as half empty, on the other hand, may grow up to be serious, analytical scientists. Many of these nine basic temperament traits have similarities to the big five personality traits. They are the beginnings of personality, and in large part they are genetically determined.

Each infant's unique set of genes determines the child's enduring characteristics and his or her general ways of reacting, thinking, and feeling. This does not mean that genes decide what someone's career will be when he or she grows up or how honest a child will become. It means that certain ways of responding to the world tend to remain stable over time—not because of what parents did during infancy but because of the genes with which the child is born.

Genes and Function

Every human being has about 20,500 genes, with half inherited from each parent. During the process of reproduction and fertilization, new combinations of genes are produced. This is known as "gene shuffling" and ensures that genetic variation occurs and that each person is a unique individual. Genes in the human population (and in every population) also have variant forms. These variants are the result of genetic mutations. The mutations occur as slight errors as the genes in a single cell (or fertilized egg) are being copied so that the cell can divide and grow into a multi-celled fetus. Some mutations cause slight changes in the way the gene functions. Scientists estimate that each person carries between five hundred and two thousand mutations, inherited from his or her ancestors. They also estimate that at least 50 percent of human genes have variants. These variants are one way that

Although infants do not have completely formed personalities, even at this young age they are already distinct individuals. Personality develops as a baby's inborn temperament and other genetic traits combine with life experiences.

people can be different from one another. For example, gene variants are why people have different blood types.

Variants in genes may slightly alter the ways in which those genes work. Genes code for proteins, and proteins do the work of the body. Each gene has some effect on the body's cells, such as causing the synthesis of a protein that is used in the cells, including brain cells. Variants in genes can change the structure of the protein that is made, and that can change how the cells work. Genetic variations produce differences in human traits such as eye color, height, hair color, and even brain function, such as with intelligence or creativity. However, to use height as an example, people do not come in just two size types—short and tall. Heights vary along a continuum, from short to medium to tall and everything in between. Some genes slightly change the coding for growth such that different adult heights are the result. In the same way, genes that code for brain cell functioning are responsible for slight changes in learning ability, temperament, and personality

Do Animals Have Personalities?

Scientists have discovered that animals of many species not only have personalities but often demonstrate personality traits similar to those found in humans. In one study, biologist Lee Dugatkin put sixty guppies in one side of a fish tank that had a glass partition down the middle. On the other side of the partition was a predator fish that eats guppies. Dugatkin discovered that guppies' behavior varies when they see a predator. Some will be very wary or worried and stay far away from the predator. Some are just medium in wariness. Some are low in wariness and willing to swim quite close to the predator. The varying levels of fearfulness about predators seems to suggest that animals, like people, are born with different personality traits, perhaps not unlike the varying levels of neuroticism in people.

Samuel D. Gosling and Oliver P. John examined nineteen different behavioral studies of twelve different animals and concluded that they could see individual differences in both neuroticism and extraversion in guppies, octopuses, chimpanzees, other primates, and mammals like cats and dogs. Some of the animals displayed behaviors that seemed remarkably similar to the behaviors seen in people with the same personality traits. People who test low in extraversion, for instance, might prefer to stay at home or remain in the background at a party. Similarly, an octopus that is low in extraversion might stay in its den, even when eating, and try to hide more often than other octopuses by releasing a cloud of ink. Sociability (extraversion), fearfulness (neuroticism), curiosity (openness), and affection and preference for closeness to their owners (agreeableness) also vary in cats and dogs. And a mathematical analysis of chimpanzee behaviors suggests that all five personality traits vary in the species. In conscientiousness, for instance, varying degrees of attention, goal-directed behavior, and impulse control can be identified in individual chimps.

dimensions. No one is irritable or calm all the time or outgoing and active all the time. There is no single way of thinking, just as there is no one type of personality. There are continuums of responses in the brain that produce individual tendencies in responsiveness to the world.

Psychological researchers theorize that multiple genes combine to determine degrees of temperament and personality traits in each individual. These genes are probably determining variations in brain responsiveness, just as genes determine variations in height. Although science has not found any specific genes related to personality, some evidence of variations in how individual brains react to different situations has been found. For example, many studies have identified a connection between extraversion and increased activity in the area of the brain known as the amygdala. The amygdala is part of the brain's limbic system, which is responsible for emotions and memory.

In one study, researcher Turhan Canli examined the emotional reactions of people to positive, happy situations, such as pictures of cute puppies or smiling, joyful people. The test subjects looked at the pictures while they lay in a magnetic resonance imaging scanner that measured the responsiveness of their brains to the images. People who were extraverted showed more activity in the amygdala than people lower on the dimension. The conclusion from this and other studies is that extraverted people enjoy positive emotions more than people low on extraversion. Their brains are built to respond highly to the pleasure of positive experiences. Canli notes, "It's interesting to imagine the mechanisms in the brain that support this desire for what seems to be a pleasant experience, and how they differ from one person to another."[5] He believes that much of this difference in brain function is genetically based. He and his research associates have identified at least one gene variant that seems to change the responsiveness of the amygdala to emotional stimulation.

> **WORDS IN CONTEXT**
>
> **amygdala**
> An almond-shaped brain structure located in the temporal lobe that processes many emotions, such as fear, anger, and pleasure.

Identical Twins, Identical Genes

Other research that supports the idea that personality is genetically based involves studies of twins. Identical twins have almost identical genes. For many years researchers have studied the

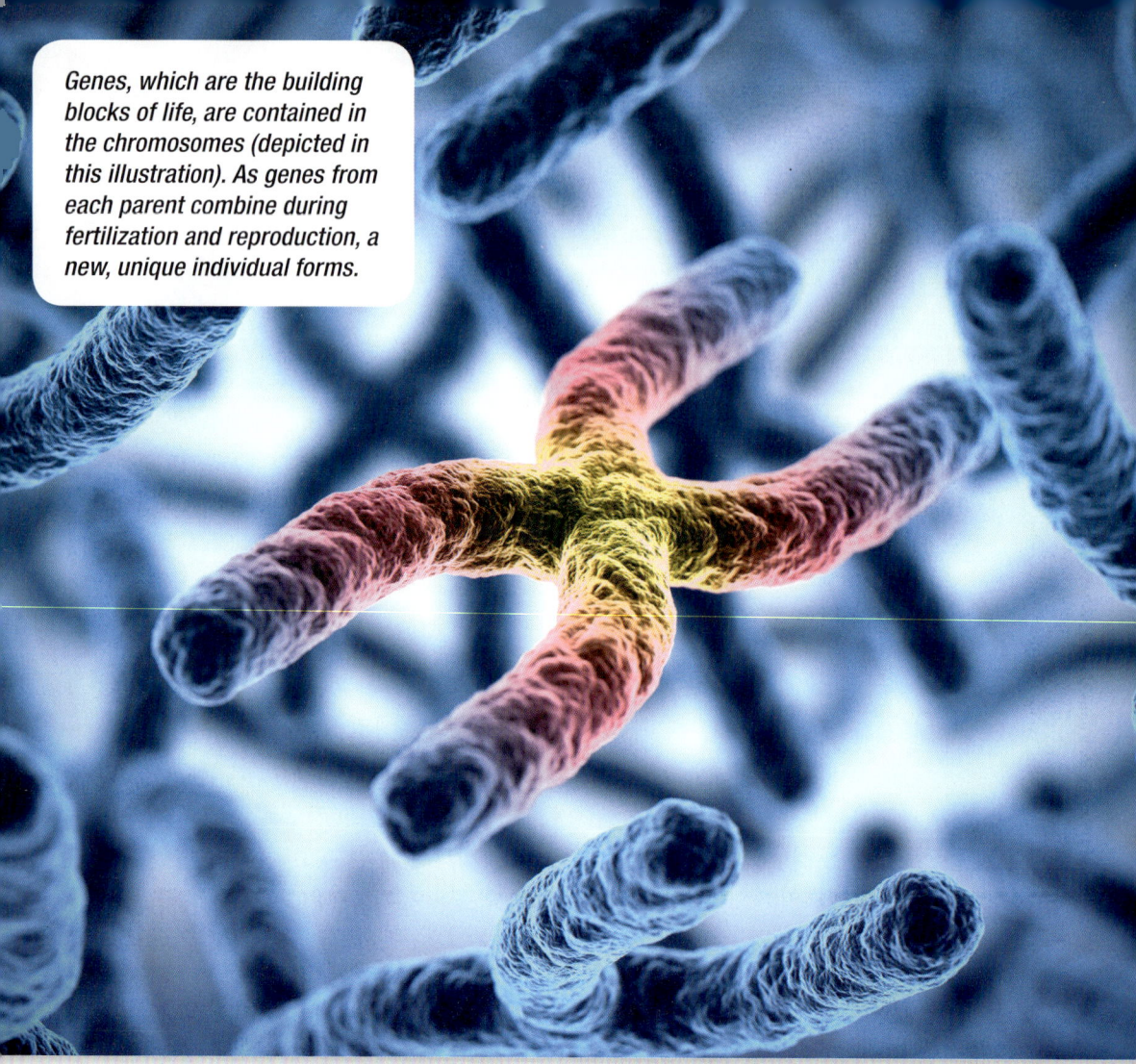

Genes, which are the building blocks of life, are contained in the chromosomes (depicted in this illustration). As genes from each parent combine during fertilization and reproduction, a new, unique individual forms.

similarities between identical twins and how twins' personality traits correlate with each other. Correlation is association and is a measure of how much two variables are related. For instance, researchers ask if one twin is low in extraversion, how likely is it that the other is also low in extraversion. Correlation is measured from 0 to 1, with 0 meaning there is no association at all and 1 meaning the relationship is perfect. Correlation is not the same as causation. It just means that two things tend to happen together. In reality, no correlation is perfect; even identical twins do not have exactly the same personalities. However, identical twins have been compared to nonidentical (fraternal) twins and to siblings who grow up together in the same family. Twins have also been studied when they are raised in different families (perhaps because they were adopted separately). Mathematically, researchers always find high correlations in identical twin personalities that do not exist in nonidentical siblings. Since identical twins share the same genes while siblings share only 50 percent, the only explanation for the differences in correlations must be genes, not the environment.

In a study of more than eight hundred pairs of twins, Timothy Bates and his research team at the University of Edinburgh compared the personality traits of identical adult twins and fraternal twins. All the twin pairs had been raised in the same families. The research team discovered that the identical twins were twice as likely to have some of the same traits as were nonidentical twins. Identical twins, for example, were particularly likely to have the same amount of self-control, feelings of well-being and optimism, and social abilities. Bates says of the results of the study, "Previously, the role of family and the environment around the home often dominated people's ideas about what affected psychological wellbeing. However, this work highlights a much more powerful influence from genetics."[6]

Since 1979 groups of researchers have been studying and analyzing information gathered from the ongoing Minnesota Twin Family Study. It includes 137 pairs of twins who were separated from birth and reared apart, with no contact with each other. Eighty-one of the pairs were identical twins, and fifty-six were fraternal. As with twins raised together, researchers have repeatedly determined that the identical twins' personalities correlate significantly with one another, while fraternal twins do not. Nancy Segal, a psychologist at California State University–Fullerton, spent nine years researching the personality characteristics of the Minnesota twins. In 2014 she reported on her findings, saying, "We were surprised by certain behaviors that showed a genetic influence, such as religiosity

> **WORDS IN CONTEXT**
>
> **correlation**
> A statistical measure of how often two or more variables tend to occur together; correlation is not the same as causation.

[and] social attitudes. Those surprised us, because we thought those certainly must come from the family."[7] Segal emphasizes that twin studies do not indicate that family and environment are unimportant in the development of personality. But she does say that genes and environment are always working together to determine personality and individual traits.

Environment Is Important, Too

Even for identical twins, genetic influences account for only about half of personality development. The differences in identical twins suggest that the environment interacts with genetic temperaments to yield stable personality traits. How this interaction occurs and which environmental influences matter is still largely unknown and is the subject of much theorizing among psychologists. Nevertheless, several environmental and early nurturing influences are thought to be critical in the development of personality. Psychological opinion is that these environmental influences occur in infancy and early childhood.

One influence that has been investigated is parenting style. Psychologists identify four parenting styles. Some parents have an authoritative style and are both firm in their expectations and supportive of their children. Some parents are neglectful and uninvolved. Some have a permissive style, which is nurturing and loving but indulgent. Some parents are authoritarian (not authoritative) and are strict, demanding, and not very supportive. All four of these styles interact with the child's inborn temperament and may affect how the child's personality develops. For example, an overly strict, authoritarian parent may cause some children to develop low self-esteem and become fearful or shy. A child from an extremely permissive environment, on the other hand, may grow up to have problems with authority or even become insecure from never having a sense of structure and rules. A child with a soft, easygoing temperament may be crushed by a strict style or become an underachiever

Identical twins often exhibit many of the same personality traits when it comes to self-control, optimism, and social skills. These shared traits may result from the fact that identical twins have nearly identical genes.

when treated too permissively. But a child with an active, outgoing temperament might rebel against the strict parents or take advantage of permissive parents.

Psychologists and child development experts also theorize that interactions between the parent's personality and the child's temperament can affect personality development, especially if the child's temperament clashes with the parent's expectations. How well parent and child fit together may affect the child's ultimate personality. Needlman explains, "For example, one parent describes her active, intense, quick-witted and strong-willed two-year-old as 'exhausting,' while another parent, whose own temperament is more compatible, calls him 'my little sparkler.'"[8] It is easy to imagine how differently a child's personality might develop if he or she is viewed as difficult rather than a joy.

Environment Before Birth

Scientists have a bit of evidence that the environment of the mother's womb may affect the infant's personality or temperament once it is born. Some researchers have reported that when a pregnant woman experiences severe stress in connection with war or the death of a loved one, for instance, her baby is likely to be more vulnerable to developing psychological disorders. Animal studies suggest that the mother's release of stress hormones can affect the developing fetus and increase its anxiety levels after birth. Other studies have found some differences in personality traits depending on the season that the infant is born. In northern Europe, for example, babies born in fall and winter (after growing as fetuses during the summer) were more likely to be more extraverted than those born in spring and summer. Scientists speculate that babies born after a summer of the mother eating well and feeling good and healthy because of the warm weather have somehow been signaled that life is positive. No one is certain about the truth of these ideas. Scientists who have attempted to study the effects of the mother's stress on her developing baby are unable to find very strong or meaningful associations as yet. Researchers say that much more investigation is necessary, and so far, little is known about the prenatal influences on personality.

Other environmental influences that researchers have explored include birth order (with firstborns seeming to be achievers and leaders, and youngest children often more spontaneous, easygoing, and a little irresponsible); early childhood illnesses or accidents that might have long-term effects; and of course, outright abuse, neglect, and other early trauma. Under severe circumstances, even a child with a positive, easygoing temperament might develop negativity, hostility, or serious emotional distress and worry. As yet, researchers have not been able to provide consistent, certain scientific evidence that these environmental influences are the ones that interact with genes to create an individual's enduring personality, but researchers and therapists who work with adult and child clients believe it is probable that they do.

From Childhood to Adulthood

Researchers do know, however, that by about age six or seven, the child's personality is pretty much set for life. In one study, psychologist Christopher Nave compared how teachers had rated the personalities of grade school children to his own personality tests and interviews with the same individuals forty years later. Nave discovered, for example, that children who had been rated as talkative and outgoing were still extraverted, social, and leadership oriented as adults. Children with low self-esteem usually grew up to be insecure adults. Nave comments, "We remain recognizably the same person. This speaks to the importance of understanding personality because it does follow us wherever we go across time and contexts."[9] Personality determinants matter for an entire lifetime, so researchers continue to explore how environment and heredity combine to produce an enduring personality.

CHAPTER 2

What Are Different Personality Styles and Traits?

No one has a personality "type." In the past many doctors did label the way people respond to stress in terms of types. For instance, "type A personality" describes an individual who is highly competitive, has an extreme work ethic, and is prone to high blood pressure and stress-related illnesses. Today, however, doctors and personality researchers do not use terms like this. Instead they say that people vary widely along a continuum of each of the big five personality traits, which combine in different ways to determine individual personalities. The resulting dimensions and styles of personality can be understood and used to broadly predict individual reactions and behaviors. For example, someone who is high on the extraversion dimension but low on the agreeableness dimension may be predicted to be very social and love to party but also quick to get into arguments with others at a party and likely to make enemies in social situations. Most people have a balance of traits and dimensions, but higher and lower tendencies on one or more of the big five traits can say a lot about how a person lives life. Each big five trait—extraversion, agreeableness, neuroticism, conscientiousness, and openness—describes interesting and meaningful aspects of human personality characteristics.

Extraversion

A person with a high level on the extraversion dimension is generally outgoing, gregarious, enthusiastic, and optimistic about life. An extravert loves seeking life's rewards, whether social status, interpersonal interactions, financial success, fame, or any other high-value goal. Extraverts get a lot of satisfaction from their endeavors. They enjoy traveling and exploring, socializing, romantic pursuits, taking risks, and aiming high in life. Extraverts have a lot of positive emotions. Personality researchers theorize that extraverts have brains that are more rewarded by pleasurable outcomes than other people. That is why extraverts are action-oriented, outward-looking, reward-seeking individuals. Many successful businesspeople, marketing executives, and chief executive officers are extraverts. Extraverts have leadership qualities and the energy and social skills to make other people in a group follow their lead.

In other situations, extraverts are go-getters, too. They may explore the world to seek new experiences or work hard to achieve the fame, fortune, and applause given to a rock star. They may become talented, professional athletes. They enjoy being the center of attention and being admired by others, and they like being included in social settings and getting to interact with everyone they meet. Extraverts enjoy life's challenges and testing themselves.

Bill (not his real name) is an example of an extraverted entrepreneur described by British psychologist Daniel Nettle. With energy, hard work, and a drive to succeed, Bill made millions of dollars before he turned forty. Then, through his enthusiasm for exploration and risk taking, he lost it all and ended up working as a ski instructor. But Bill is not discouraged by his seeming failure. Instead he remains optimistic and excited about working his way back to being rich and successful again. He is sure he can do it and looks forward to the challenge. Bill says, "There is nothing better than to win a struggle. I love taking risks."[10]

Extraversion, however, can lead to taking too many risks. Nettle did a study of people hospitalized for accidents and injuries, for instance, and discovered that they were likely to rank higher on the extraversion dimension than those hospitalized for other reasons. Sometimes extraverts take too many risks and perhaps are overly optimistic about their abilities. Some studies have found that extraverts are more likely to die at younger ages than are other people.

Extraverts are generally outgoing, gregarious, and optimistic. They seek out adventure and thrive on action, risk, and reward.

Nettle says, "The researchers attribute part of this to more drinking and smoking [risk taking], and the rest to some unidentified lifestyle factor, which I would bet is rushing around pursuing thrilling rewards."[11]

Thrilling rewards and excitement are not particularly valuable to those who rank at low levels on the dimension of extraversion. The opposite of extraversion is introversion. Contrary to popular opinion, introverts are not shy, withdrawn, or depressed people. Rather, they are calm, quiet, somewhat aloof or detached people, whose brains do not react as strongly to positive emotions. They have positive emotions and enjoy them, but they are not so excited by such emotions that they need to pursue them enthusiastically. They are not as rewarded by socialization, social interactions, and life's extrinsic rewards as are extraverts. Several studies suggest that an introvert's brain is more sensitive to the brain chemical dopamine than extraverts. Dopamine is released in the brain in response to pleasurable occurrences and rewards. Both introverts and extraverts have the same amount of dopamine in the brain, but being more sensitive to it means that it can feel like too much. Instead of being charged up by an exciting rock concert, for example, the introvert may feel overstimulated and need time alone after all that excitement. Extraverts are energized by social contacts, while introverts may be tired out. Introverts are not antisocial; they just need less social contact and experiences. They enjoy peacefulness, calmness, and solitude rather than constant stimulation.

Introverts are often calmly satisfied with life and can take things as they come, but they can be quite motivated and successful in careers, too. They can focus and concentrate on goals, and they can be thoughtful leaders and good listeners. They can work on projects alone rather than needing the energy of a group. Susan Cain, who has written books on introversion, says, "Introverted leaders often possess an innate caution that may be more valuable than we realize."[12] Microsoft founder Bill Gates says that he is an example of an introvert. He argues that his introversion is why he is comfortable being alone and quietly thinking through problems.

Conscientiousness

High or low extraversion, however, is only one dimension that influences any kind of success in life. Conscientiousness is the dimension associated with impulse control. People who have a high level of conscientiousness are self-controlled, self-disciplined, and able to be goal directed. Such people have a good work ethic and consider others when making a decision. People who have low levels of conscientiousness may be impulsive, spontaneous, and lacking in the self-control to give up an immediate reward (like a party) to attain a long-term reward (like an A in a class). Most people are somewhere in the middle when it comes to conscientiousness. They are sometimes self-controlled and sometimes give in to the impulse to have fun. However, high or low conscientiousness can have significant effects on lifestyle choices.

Highly conscientious people are always making plans and thinking ahead. They set goals and stick to them and are not distracted by immediate pleasures or interesting alternatives. These approaches can have positive consequences in the workplace, for saving funds for a special vacation trip or buying a house, or in earning a college degree. But there are disadvantages to being extremely conscientious, too. It is difficult for highly conscientious people to be spontaneous, and sometimes spontaneous, impulsive behavior is both fun and appropriate. Socially, people who are extremely conscientious may be overly perfectionistic or seem boring to others.

Microsoft founder Bill Gates (pictured) describes himself as an introvert. Introverts tend to be calm, thoughtful, and able to focus on their goals.

At the other extreme, people with low levels of conscientiousness may be fun to be with, but they may fail to consider the consequences of their actions. They are often liable to procrastinate on tasks and to describe themselves as lazy. A lack of impulse control, combined with extraverted willingness to take risks, also can be a primary cause of drug addiction, gambling problems, and an inability to stop behaviors that damage the individual or other people. (Extraverts with high levels of conscientiousness may experiment but can decide to stop the behavior if it becomes problematic.) Impulsiveness is the opposite of conscientiousness, and psychologists believe that addictions are related to being unable to inhibit, or stop, an activity that was pleasurable in the past. Most impulsive people do not become addicts, but being unable to inhibit an activity is a risk factor for addiction and an inability to break bad habits.

Scientists have determined that there are differences in brain functioning between conscientious and impulsive people. In a study comparing brain structures to different personality dimensions, researcher Colin DeYoung of the University of Minnesota determined that conscientious people have a larger lateral prefrontal cortex than impulsive ones. The lateral prefrontal cortex is particularly responsible for planning, goal setting, and following rules. In conscientious people, DeYoung theorizes, this area of the brain may be larger because it has grown and changed with an individual's experiences and behaviors. In brain imaging studies, conscientious people also show greater activity in this area of the brain than do impulsive people when they are engaged in tasks that require them to inhibit responses.

> **WORDS IN CONTEXT**
>
> **cortex**
> The outer layer of the gray matter of the brain's hemispheres that plays a large role in consciousness and higher functioning.

Neuroticism

DeYoung's research found an area of the prefrontal cortex related to the dimension of neuroticism, too. It is an area that helps regulate emotions and is smaller in people with very high levels of neuroticism as compared to those with low levels. Again, researchers such as DeYoung do not know if this size is innate or if it occurs because of reactions to experience that change how the brain develops. Neuroticism is the dimension related to emotional stability. Generally, people with high levels on this dimension are worriers. Most people are a little high or a little low in levels of neuroticism, and that is actually a good thing. Never worrying over anything could lead to a lot of trouble, while having very high levels of neuroticism could mean much sadness and anxiety.

People lower on the continuum are generally secure, comfortable with themselves, and unlikely to stress over too many things. As people move higher on the continuum, their responsiveness to negative emotions increases. Just as extraverts respond strongly to pictures of happy faces, brain imaging studies show that those with high levels of neuroticism react more strongly to negative scenarios. The amygdala is involved in this reactivity, the same as it is for the positive emotions of extraverts.

People with high levels of neuroticism are sensitive to all kinds of negative emotions, such as sadness, anxiety, shame, guilt, fear, and depression. They can be extremely shy, which is basically a fear of social judgment. They can do a lot of worrying about whether they are good people or whether they are making the right decisions about their lives. They may lie awake at night worrying about what might happen or what has already happened. Where others might interpret events as being of small importance, high-neuroticism people see the same events in extremes. Nettle explains the different statements that people on this continuum might use to respond to negative experiences. His examples include, "'It was all my fault,' 'Everybody hates me,' 'I will never succeed,' versus 'I did my best but circumstances were against me,' 'Those people are misguided,' 'It will go better next time.'"[13]

Individuals who have very high levels on the neuroticism dimension are more likely than others to suffer from depression, anxiety disorders, post-traumatic stress, and phobias. This is because they often direct their negative emotions toward themselves, feeling constant doubt about their worth. On the surface, it seems as if having high levels of neuroticism has no redeeming

Being Funny

In 2009 researchers Gil Greengross and Geoffrey F. Miller published a study of the personality traits of stand-up comedians. Many people think that comedians are sad clowns or neurotic individuals who deal with the stress of life by making jokes. The researchers found that this characterization was false. Compared to noncomedian college students, both amateur and professional comedians were high in openness and lower in agreeableness, extraversion, and conscientiousness. They were no different from other people on neuroticism. Greengross and Miller were surprised by this finding, since other creative people are often high in neuroticism. The researchers speculate that the difference is that comedians have to perform in public. In the highly competitive business of stand-up comedy, the comedians have to be emotionally stable in order to perform in front of an audience, be nonanxious about the performance, and control the flow of their acts.

features, but that is not true. Many studies have shown, for example, that novelists, poets, and artists are much more likely than others to suffer from depression, yet their talents and value are immense. Interestingly, unhappy people also see the world more realistically than do happy people. People such as the playwright Henrik Ibsen or the novelist Fyodor Dostoevsky have greatly contributed to our understanding of society, humankind's condition, and the need to right the world's wrongs. They were often unhappy and no doubt ranked high on the neuroticism dimension, but they offered insights and the incentives to improve social systems that happy, contented people could never supply.

Agreeableness

People who have high levels of neuroticism often feel distressed when they learn about other people's suffering, but interestingly, that sorrow goes only so far without a high level of agreeableness as well. In 2016 Meara Habashi and her research team did a study of personality traits and empathy. The psychologists attempted to measure how strongly their test subjects reacted to different scenarios of strangers in trouble. Subjects high in neuroticism experienced a great deal of emotional distress upon hearing about people needing help. They were sympathetic and sorry, but it was the subjects high in agreeableness who actually tried to help. Agreeableness is the dimension of empathy and the tendency to care about the emotional and mental states of other people. Those with high levels of agreeableness are trusting, caring, cooperative, and invested in interpersonal relationships. Psychologists label the desire to help others "prosocial behavior." This does not mean wanting to socialize but caring about the social good. People with high levels of agreeableness are prosocial. They are likely to value family and friends more than career success, volunteer their time for the greater good, donate to charity, give blood, or stop and help a sick stranger on a busy street. They often choose helping professions, such as teaching and social work. In sum, they are nice, friendly people who enjoy pleasing others.

At the other end of the continuum, disagreeable people are often described as cold, critical, aggressive, less trusting, and selfish. One man who is both introverted and low in agreeableness says, "I find human company rather boring most of the time. I prefer to be on my own, so that I have the freedom to let my thoughts go the way I want them to."[14] He also says that he sees no reason to change because he is not hurting anyone with his lack of interest. This man is a good husband and father, but he gets no pleasure out of prosocial activities.

Having a high level of agreeableness seems like a good trait, and indeed, some studies suggest highly agreeable people are happier than others, but a bit of disagreeableness can be a positive thing at times. For instance, those with lower levels of agreeableness are often more successful and make more money than highly agreeable people. Psychologist Art Markman explains why

WORDS IN CONTEXT

interpersonal
Related to the relationships, interactions, and communication between people.

People with high levels of agreeableness often choose helping professions such as teaching. They are likely to place high value on interpersonal relationships and on working for the social good.

"nice guys finish last" in the business world and why achieving business success can mean having to be selfish. He says, "Good leaders need to be able to tell people things that they do not want to hear. And honestly, putting yourself forward for a promotion means putting yourself before others."[15]

Openness

Where an individual falls on the agreeableness continuum may predict some kinds of business successes, but another kind of success is predicted by openness. Artists and poets have particularly high levels of openness. Openness refers to being open to new and unusual ideas, feelings, and behaviors. Open individuals enjoy fantasies, aesthetic experiences, and exploring novel ideas and unconventional values. They may be attracted to the spiritual and mystical, but not necessarily religion in the traditional sense. They search for meaning in socially unorthodox religious systems or New Age ideas. And they prefer the nonconventional in politics and social systems, as well. They often report interest and experiences with the paranormal or in extrasensory perception.

People with high levels of openness are imaginative and creative and enjoy culturally intellectual pursuits, but openness is the dimension least understood by personality researchers, so it can be hard to define. Some psychologists, for example, believe that open individuals are creative in all intellectual areas. Other researchers believe that creativity in mathematics and the sciences is not related to openness and is different from creativity in the arts. Practical problem solvers who do not like speculative, mystical ideas might be highly creative in their field but have low levels of openness. People with very low levels of openness tend to prefer the conventional, the traditional, and routines rather than variety.

As with every big five trait, no level of openness is either right or wrong. Open people may see conventional people as dull, boring, and stuck in a rut. People with low levels of openness may see highly open people as weird, eccentric, disruptive, or outright crazy. With every big five dimension, there are people at the extremes of the continuum and many just higher or lower on the traits. Just the fact that a person can have high or low levels on each of these five broad dimensions means that there are forty-five possible combinations that can be identified and measured. High or low extraversion can combine with high or low openness, and high or low neuroticism, and so on, for all the five factors. Yet even these generalizations can fail to describe a single individual accurately. The five-factor model is just a starting point for researchers trying to understand what a complete personality truly is.

CHAPTER 3

What Can Be Learned from Personality Tests?

Psychologists sometimes use personality tests to determine an individual personality style or profile. This testing, or assessment, is done with a variety of self-reporting questionnaires. The tests rely on questions or statements that are designed to find out how people describe themselves. Sometimes, these series of statements are rated by another person who knows the individual well. For example, a teacher might rate a student on the descriptions, or a friend might rate a friend on the statements. Personality tests vary in length, in the types of statements used, and in how accurately they describe an individual, but all have the same basic goal. That is to determine a personality profile for the individual being tested and to ascertain the dimensions and traits that define his or her personality.

How Personality Testing Works

One of the most respected personality tests used for research today is the Big Five Inventory (BFI) developed by Oliver P. John and his research team at the University of California–Berkeley in 1998. The BFI consists of forty-four statements, groups of which are designed to measure where the test taker falls on the continuum of each of the five personality factors. Each test taker self-reports how much each statement is true about him- or herself on a scale from "strongly disagree" to "strongly agree." For example, statements related to extraversion/introversion might be, "I see myself as someone who is talkative" (usually associated with extraversion) or "I see myself as someone who is reserved"[16] (usually associated with introversion). People taking tests such as the BFI are reassured at the outset that no response is correct or incorrect because there are no traits that are right or wrong. Test takers are encouraged to answer each descriptive phrase honestly if they want honest results.

Once a test subject has completed all the statements, a professional scores the test and then assigns a rating score for each personality dimension. For example, a person might score low on extraversion, very high on agreeableness, high on conscientiousness, high on neuroticism, and somewhat high on openness. The professional scorer would use these ratings to determine general statements about the individual that describe basic personality traits and which traits might dominate the personality. In this example, the person would be described as relatively introverted and comfortable in social situations with close friends rather than in large groups; he or she would also enjoy spending time alone and likely be reserved and quiet in public situations. This individual would be friendly, warm, trusting, sympathetic, and cooperative (agreeable); organized, reliable, and self-disciplined (conscientious); and more emotional than most people, often feeling anxious or worrying about things (neuroticism). Probably this individual would feel shy, self-conscious, and insecure a lot of the time. Finally, he or she would be considered somewhat open to new experiences and creative endeavors, enjoying the exploration of new ideas and finding them relatively easy to learn.

Whether a test taker is high, very high, or extremely high on a dimension is determined by comparing the person's scores to the scores of other test takers. The scores are measured in terms of percentiles. For example, a 94 percent score on extraversion indicates that the individual scores higher on extraversion than 94 percent of the population. That is extremely high extraversion. A percentile of 60, however, would be somewhat high, while one of 49 would be about average. Psychologists know what the percentiles are for the population because the BFI has been given to many thousands of people throughout the world.

Why Test Personality?

Knowing an individual's personality profile is especially useful to researchers who study human behavior and decision making. For instance, psychologist Samuel D. Gosling studied how preferences for types of music relate to personality dimensions. One of the things he discovered is that people who like funk, hip-hop, rap, soul, and electronic music are more extraverted than people who like other musical styles.

Other researchers have discovered that being high in neuroticism and also high in conscientiousness can be a good thing. Psychologist Nicholas A. Turiano's research team, for example, concluded that there are people who are "healthy neurotics." They

Personality testing has shown that someone who has high levels of both conscientiousness and neuroticism may actually outperform others in the workplace as well as make good decisions in their personal lives.

actually have fewer chronic diseases, healthier body weights, and fewer chemical and hormonal signs of stress and inflammation. In the workplace, too, people high in conscientiousness and neuroticism do well, even though they are anxious worriers. Turiano says, "Those high in conscientiousness may have anxiety but it is not making the person freeze while they ruminate on their life problems. They act on their anxiety and that is what motivates them to address what they have anxiety about [such as good health]." As for work performance, Turiano adds, "The healthy neurotic individuals somehow find a way to channel that anxiety they have to motivate them to do good work."[17] Turiano and other researchers learn from studies like this why some neurotic people function better than others, and they hope in the future to learn how to help different kinds of people make healthier choices.

Psychologists and therapists may find personality profiles useful, too. Knowing a client's personality profile can help the therapist figure out the best counseling approach for that person. For example, short-term group therapy to help individuals overcome severe grief has been found to help some kinds of personalities better than others. An individual who is extraverted, open, and conscientious does well with this kind of supportive group therapy and feels better. An individual high in neuroticism does less well and tends to benefit more from individual therapy.

Craig Lounsbrough is a family counselor who uses personality testing with his clients and shares the results with them. He explains that teaching good communication skills to families in trouble is an important part of his job. And he says:

Personality profiles shed light on various communication styles and how differing individuals may be clashing or not connecting. This information is particularly helpful in family and couples counseling. Not only does it explain many of the difficulties relative to communication, [but] it allows individuals to understand those differences and make sense of them. I have found many individuals obtaining a tremendous amount of relief in simply understanding the barriers to their communication.[18]

Tried but Not True

The Myers-Briggs Type Indicator (MBTI) is a widely used personality test. Millions of people have taken the test to find out their presumed personality type. Many businesses use the test with prospective employees to determine whether the person is a good fit for the company. Yet for psychologists, it is highly controversial. The MBTI tests for four dimensions that are similar to but not the same as five-factor personality tests. When scored, it yields sixteen personality types. Personality researchers say the test results are not reliable. An estimated 75 percent of test takers score a different personality type when they retake the test. It is not particularly valid either. The National Academy of Sciences reviewed twenty different research studies of the MBTI and reports that the test compares poorly with five-factor tests of personality traits. The types being measured by the MBTI do not seem to be mathematically meaningful, and the categories have not been statistically determined to be separate, distinct traits. Other research studies have determined that the personality types do not correlate with any particular job qualifications nor predict career success. For serious scientists working in the field of psychology, the MBTI is useless, despite its popularity. Psychologist Todd Essig says, "The MBTI is pretty much nonsense, sciencey snake oil. As is well-established by research, it has no more reliability and validity than a good Tarot card reading."

Todd Essig, "The Mysterious Popularity of the Meaningless Myers-Briggs (MBTI)," *Forbes*, September 29, 2014. www.forbes.com.

Many people who may not need any kind of counseling take personality tests just so they can learn more about themselves. Individuals often like to have a better understanding of themselves and how they compare to other people. Some people enjoy comparing their own view of themselves to the test results. Mitch Prinstein, a psychology professor at the University of North Carolina–Chapel Hill, explains about personality tests: "Ultimately, they give you some feedback on whether your behavior is similar to others, what your niche is, and how similar you are to a sub-group of people. That is inherently very rewarding to people."[19]

Meaningful Measures of Personality

In the field of psychology and psychological research, there are several respected five-factor personality tests besides the BFI. These tests are similar to the BFI, but they may vary by how the questions or statements are written or in how they are scored. Some, such as the NEO Personality Inventory or the International Personality Item Pool-NEO, are long and detailed, consisting of two hundred to three hundred statements. Statements may be about loving large parties, getting angry easily, and making friends easily. These detailed tests are mainly used by trained professionals for research or in therapy situations. Other tests—such as the New-castle Personality Assessor, which has only twelve questions—are quite short. These tests are used for a quick assessment of personality when time is an issue and it is not as important that the results be completely accurate. In general, the more questions a test has, the more likely it is to produce an accurate personality profile. No personality test, however, is always accurate for every person all the time. This is because personality profiles are based on averages for groups of people, and not every individual may interpret every question in the same way or fit into the group norms.

Generally, psychologists consider standard personality tests based on the big five to be meaningful measures of personality, but not all personality tests are created equal. Many tests that purport to measure personality and traits appear in popular magazines or on the Internet, but most of these tests are just for fun. They may not provide accurate and reliable information because they have not been researched and standardized appropriately. Psychologists depend on five-factor model tests that have been extensively researched to achieve acceptable personality profiles. They have determined that these tests are both reliable and valid.

> **WORDS IN CONTEXT**
>
> **reliability**
> A measure of a test's consistency.

The Importance of Reliability and Validity

Reliability refers to how consistently a test yields the same results. For a test to be reliable, it must give generally the same score if an individual takes it a second time. This is known as test-retest reliability. If the results of testing and retesting are vastly different, the test is not measuring anything very meaningful or stable. Another way to measure a test's reliability is to ask different professionals to administer and score the same test; their ratings of the test taker should be generally the same as well. Once a test is determined to be reliable, researchers can also check for reliability of a different personality test by comparing results on that test to the test known to be reliable. For example, psychologist Samuel D. Gosling developed a short personality measure named the Ten Item Personality Inventory (TIPI). It has only two questions for measuring each of the five personality dimensions. Gosling used test-retest reliability and compared TIPI results to results for the same individuals on other standard personality tests to check for reliability of his short assessment. Gosling determined that the TIPI is reliable enough to be useful, but he says, "Compared with standard multi-item measures of the Big Five, the TIPI is less reliable."[20] That is a warning to researchers that the results for some individuals will not be as trustworthy as with longer tests.

Gosling also found that the TIPI is not statistically as valid as longer tests. *Validity* refers to how true a test is. Does it measure what it is supposed to measure? As an example, one might ask if statements about sociability, talkativeness, and enthusiasm really measure extraversion. Assessments such as the BFI and the NEO Personality Inventory have been statistically analyzed repeatedly to be sure that they measure the five personality factors. (The TIPI is a valid measure more often than not, but it has nowhere near the statistical validity of these longer tests for all test takers.)

Researchers have also studied how often people lie or fake responses to the test statements and found that the large majority of test takers answer honestly. Even when tests are given as a condition of employment, only about one in seven people rate themselves dishonestly. Other studies compare individu-

The validity of personality testing depends on many factors. But overall, researchers have found that people usually answer questions honestly and that one's mood on the day of testing has little effect on the results.

al personality profiles to interview descriptions of people who know the individual well. The researcher asks whether these other people see the individual as low in agreeableness descriptions or high in extraversion descriptions. Close relatives or friends of the test taker are not asked to fill out the test statements; they are asked about the actual traits that the test taker exhibits.

The Stability of Personality Profiles

Researchers have also studied how valid and reliable personality testing results are over time. If the big five dimensions are stable traits and the tests are truly measuring basic personality, then personality profiles should not change even when the tests are taken years apart. Psychologists want to know if the way people describe themselves is dependent on their present situation. What if the test taker is in a bad mood that day or won the lottery the previous week? Would the individual change his or her self-report about personality characteristics? Many studies have addressed this issue, and repeatedly, psychologists discover that personality testing, in general, is measuring traits that are both stable and enduring. As long ago as 1980, Paul T. Costa Jr., Robert R. McCrae, and David Arenberg gave a group of adults a personality test three different times over eighteen years. The researchers discovered that resulting personality profiles remained remarkably similar from one test to the next. This did not mean that there were no changes but that the changes were small and that people did not go, for instance, from being agreeable to disagreeable or extraverted to introverted. Scores might be higher or lower for some people, but the overall traits remained quite stable. Costa and McCrae have conducted many more studies of the stability of personality, some spanning forty years. They continue to find that personality profiles are not dependent on the test taker's situation, age level, or temporary emotional status. No matter what the age of the test-taking subjects, their personalities remained very much the same over time.

Costa and McCrae, however, conducted their research with adults. From their extensive research, they have concluded that the most enduring personality is achieved in adults past age thirty. Before that age, even though basic personality trends are in place, they believe that personality is more flexible and plastic. They say, "Between 20 and 30, both men and women become somewhat less emotional and thrill-seeking and somewhat more cooperative and self-disciplined—changes we might interpret as evidence of increased maturity."[21] This does not imply that people do not change over the years after age thirty, because of course they do. It means that more often than not and in general, people respond to the world within the same broad dimensions of personality that were established early in life.

The Limitations of Personality Testing

Standard personality tests are relatively good measures of the big five personality factors and relatively good predictors of how people will react to situations and the choices they will make. However, no description of personality can take all individual differences into account. In any given situation, no test can predict how an individual will react. For example, the most introverted person may go on a talking jag once in a while; the most conscientious may cheat on a test or speed on the highway; the calmest, most emotionally stable person may become anxious or stressed in a bad situation. But over many situations, personality tests can indicate the actions and feelings that are likely to occur most frequently in an individual's life. The tests can predict the reactions that will, on average, reflect personality (worrying, thrill seeking, and so on).

To illustrate how personality can predict outcomes, psychologist Daniel Nettle gives an example of an individual low in agreeableness. Such a person in an office setting might want to use

Are Personality Traits Universal?

Many psychological researchers have attempted to determine if the big five traits apply to people in different cultures around the world. In general, the answer seems to be that, with minor variations, they do. The BFI developed by Oliver P. John has been translated into several languages, including Dutch, Chinese, Italian, Spanish, and Swedish. Researchers in different countries use these translations to study personality dimensions in their own cultures. In 2016, for example, a team of Chinese psychologists used the BFI to measure personality traits for people native to China. The team's findings were very similar to findings for American populations. Just as with other cultures, for instance, the team found that female test takers scored higher in agreeableness and neuroticism than males. And older people were more agreeable and conscientious and less neurotic and open than young people.

the copy machine or need particular pieces of equipment and find them already in use. Out of all the times that this happens, perhaps 10 percent of the time the low-agreeableness person might get irritable and snap at his or her coworker. No personality test can predict when or if this person will be disagreeable. But over the course of a year, even if the person low in agreeableness snaps irritably only once a day, that means an average of more than two hundred times a year when he or she is annoyed with coworkers. This not only affects how the person gets along at work, it is an outcome that fits a low-agreeableness personality profile. Nettle says, "The more we aggregate [sum up] behaviours across multiple instances, the more important personality as a predictor becomes."[22]

Personality testing is both valid and reliable, and it can be broadly useful, but it is not a perfect measure of any individual at any point in time. Nettle explains, "Psychology is not like physics, where you can predict the trajectory of an individual object to many decimal places. The best that any kind of psychology can hope for is *some* predictive power at the statistical level across a group of people. We will never be at the stage of making exact predictions about what individuals will do and when."[23] People just cannot be completely defined by personality tests.

CHAPTER 4

What Are Personality Disorders?

Personality profiles typically describe dimensions and variations of normal traits, reactions, and behaviors, but personality disorders are something quite different. Usually, the professionals who study personality are not the same people who diagnose and treat personality disorders. The former are researchers, while the latter are clinicians—professionals trained to be directly involved and work with patients or clients. These professionals are usually psychiatrists, psychologists, and other mental health workers. The diagnosis of a personality disorder is not so much based on scientific study as on clinical observation and theory. How personality disorders relate to five-factor personality profiles is still being investigated. Both areas of personality analysis, however, describe basic, long-lasting patterns of acting, thinking, and feeling.

Disorders Defined

Personality disorders are persistent ways of thinking, feeling, and behaving that cause significant distress or problems functioning in society. According to the American Psychiatric Association (APA), these disorders commonly begin in late adolescence or early adulthood, but the APA says clinicians cannot accurately diagnose any personality disorder at this young age unless the symptoms have been present for at least one year. Personality traits are not yet completely set in young people and may change. Furthermore, since the definition of personality disorder requires long-lasting patterns, adolescents often have not exhibited the characteristic traits long enough for such a diagnosis. Personality disorders may affect close to 10 percent of the US adult population. Researchers believe that the cause is equal parts genes and the environment, but no one as yet knows why some people develop personality disorders and others do not.

Currently, the APA recognizes ten types of personality disorders. All are considered to be primarily problems with self-identity and relationships with other people, but in different ways. All are characterized by enduring and intractable patterns in at least two of the following four areas:

- Way of thinking about oneself and others
- Way of responding emotionally
- Way of relating to other people
- Way of controlling one's behavior[24]

The ten personality disorders are grouped into three categories called clusters. The clusters are based on the similarities of the characteristics and symptoms and are labeled A, B, and C.

Cluster A Personality Disorders

Cluster A is the odd or eccentric cluster and includes three disorders. An example of a personality disorder in this cluster is paranoid personality disorder. The disorder is characterized by pervasive suspicion and mistrust of others. People with this disorder think that other people are acting on mean, spiteful motives. They worry that other people may want to harm them, put them down, or fool them in some way. They find it hard to become close to anyone or confide in other people, even family members. In society, such people seem cold and hostile; they get into arguments frequently because they are extremely sensitive to criticism and think that casual comments or looks have a hidden, threatening meaning. They are likely to hold grudges for perceived insults, act aggressively and seek revenge for imagined wrongs, and be jealous and controlling in relationships. For instance, a man might be suspicious that his girlfriend or wife is cheating on him, even though there is no evidence of unfaithfulness at all. He may be completely unable to get along with neighbors and be quick to

Someone who suffers from paranoid personality disorder is likely to be jealous and controlling in relationships. A man who has this disorder might suspect his wife or girlfriend of cheating on him even when no evidence of unfaithfulness exists.

sue them in court over property rights, noisiness, a wandering pet in his yard, or the neighbor's refusal to do anything his way. People with paranoid personality disorder think they are always right and others always wrong.

Professionals report that paranoid personality disorder is more common in men than women. It can be mild enough that the person can maintain fairly normal functioning in society most of the time, seeming just oddly suspicious and disagreeable to others, or it can be severe enough to disable the person in society. Such individuals may not be able to marry or have a close

Dangerously Disordered

After John W. Hinckley Jr. attempted to assassinate President Ronald Reagan in 1981, he was found not guilty by reason of insanity. The psychiatrists who diagnosed him mentioned multiple psychiatric disorders and mental illnesses as contributing to his legal insanity. One of those diagnoses was narcissistic personality disorder. People with narcissistic personality disorder have grandiose feelings about themselves, believe that they are unique, and have a strong need for other people to recognize how special they are. They have little to no empathy for other people and are quite willing to cheat or take credit for work not their own. They feel entitled to whatever they value and are disturbed when other people do not recognize their importance. Narcissistic personality disorder alone does not drive anyone to violence. Hinckley was also diagnosed as psychotic (with a major break from reality), depressive, and with other personality disorders. But being self-centered and self-absorbed definitely contributed to his being a danger to society. His presumed desire for fame and notoriety seemed to be caused by the narcissistic personality disorder that helped drive his actions.

personal relationship, may be unable to hold a job because they cannot get along with others, and may end up completely withdrawn from society because of their disordered thinking. Researchers estimate that between 2.3 percent and 4.4 percent of the population is affected by paranoid personality disorder, but the intensity of the symptoms usually decreases with age. By the time a person with this disorder is in his or her forties or fifties, extreme and severe symptoms start to disappear.

Cluster B Personality Disorders

Cluster B is the dramatic, erratic, and emotional cluster of four personality disorders. The disorders in this cluster include antisocial (not caring about the rights or feelings of others), histrionic (excessively emotional and attention seeking), or narcissistic (feeling extremely self-important and lacking empathy for others). However, the most common disorder in the cluster is borderline personality disorder (BPD). A person with BPD has an enduring pattern of instability in emotions, mood, and relationships. He or she often has a poor self-image, feels worthless or bad, and may indulge in impulsive, sometimes reckless, behavior as a result. The person with BPD also may suffer from excessive fear of losing relationships and being alone, thoughts of suicide, and feelings of emptiness, sadness, and despair. People with BPD are very fearful of being abandoned by a loved one and can therefore be demanding and needy and then become panicked or angry if the other person fails to seem devoted enough. BPD can cause extreme sensitivity to even mild stresses in relationships with others. For example, a woman with BPD might interpret a boyfriend having to cancel a date for a good reason as proof that he does not care about her and that she is going to be neglected and unloved forever. That can lead to feelings of emptiness, worthlessness, and even a desire to self-harm, such as by cutting, or perform other self-destructive behaviors.

Marsha M. Linehan, for example, developed borderline personality disorder as a teen, during the 1960s. She was seriously mentally ill and says now, "I was in hell."[25] She hurt herself by burning her wrists with cigarettes; cut her arms, legs, and abdomen with sharp objects; banged her head against the wall; tried to commit suicide; and felt completely out of control. Her feelings of loneliness

and emptiness were unbearable. She could not seem to get off the emotional roller coaster that kept carrying her into despair whenever she tried to cope with life. She explains about her condition, "Borderline individuals are the psychological equivalent of third-degree-burn patients. They simply have, so to speak, no emotional skin."[26] During her teens and twenties, she was hospitalized twice for self-destructive behaviors and seemed so hopeless that her doctors doubted she would survive. They thought she was untreatable and doomed to a lifelong struggle with her inner demons. At that time, no one knew how to help a person like Linehan, so she had to find her own path to recovery. And recover she did. She found her own spiritual, religious, and intellectual strengths and over time grew her own strong emotional skin. She learned to love, accept, and believe in herself. Today Linehan is a highly respected psychologist and therapist who has developed a treatment for BPD and is a spokesperson for those with the disorder.

BPD is the most studied of all the personality disorders, but it is still poorly understood. Clinicians have different opinions about the environmental factors (such as childhood abuse) that may cause the condition, whether symptoms decrease with age, and about when to diagnose it. It can be confused with other psychological illnesses and can vary enormously in severity. Studies have shown that it is often misdiagnosed (people are incorrectly diagnosed with another mental disorder) and overdiagnosed (people are diagnosed as having BPD when they do not). Researchers estimate that between 1 percent and 2 percent of the population suffer from BPD and that more females than males are affected.

Cluster C Personality Disorders

Cluster C includes three disorders characterized by anxious and fearful behavior. It includes obsessive-compulsive personality disorder (OCPD), which is not the same as obsessive-compulsive disorder (OCD). The similarity in names is confusing, but the inclusion of the term *personality* makes a big difference. Psychiatrist Fred K. Berger explains, for instance, "People with OCD have unwanted thoughts, while people with OCPD believe that their thoughts are correct. In addition, OCD often begins in childhood while OCPD usually starts in the teen years or early 20s."[27] Furthermore, people with OCD often cope with rituals such as hand washing or counting steps, while people with OCPD do not. Instead they are perfectionistic, rigid, extremely orderly, and always worried about control. The disorder can range from mild to severe, but it can be seriously disabling. For example, at work a person with OCPD can get so concerned about making every detail of a project perfect that he or she cannot ever finish the job. He or she may become so obsessed with work in general that no time is left for family, friends, or recreation. A person with OCPD experiences great anxiety and frustration when others will not accept or submit to the perfect way of doing something. OCPD is perhaps the most common personality disorder, affecting between 2.1 percent and 7.9 percent of the population. It is diagnosed in twice as many men as women.

Avoidant personality disorder is much more uncommon, affecting about 1 percent of the population. People with this disorder have an enduring pattern of feeling extremely shy, inhibited, and inadequate. They are always fearful of rejection from other people. They may lead lives of painful isolation because they fear criticism, disapproval, and loss so much that they avoid establishing relationships at all. They think about their flaws and faults continually and are extremely insecure. Avoidant personality disorder can only be diagnosed in adults because shyness and insecurity are a normal part of maturation in children and teens. The important distinction for the disorder is that it is long lasting and interferes with normal life. An Internet support website for people with avoidant personality disorder describes the severity of the disorder:

> Ultimately, we may find ways to "cope." We might decide that being alone is preferable to being with others. We may find our own company though lonely . . . safer than what we had experienced before. We think—If we don't risk then we can keep others from hurting us. If we can build walls around our hearts, around our bodies then we can cocoon and find solace within the quiet peace of ourselves. We want a soulful existence but the FEAR is strong, the vulnerability just too much and so . . . we go inward.[28]

Can Personality Disorders Be Treated?

With treatment, there is hope for people suffering the fear and pain of avoidant personality disorder and for many other types of personality disorders, even when the problems have endured for years. However, psychologists and psychiatrists say that personality disorders can be hard to treat. Treatment almost always involves intensive talk therapy, and if anxiety or depression is serious, medication may be useful as well. The first step in treatment is to help the individual come to understand that his or her difficulties are caused by patterns of thinking and feeling that are not functional or appropriate. People with personality disorders need to understand that their problems with relationships, work, and society come from disordered ways of relating to the world, and that realization can be difficult. Then, they need to learn new ways of behaving and new skills for dealing with social interactions. Even when the personality disorder cannot be cured, significant improvement in emotional health, realistic thinking about the world, and positive behavior is possible.

Some personality disorders are easier to treat than others. Paranoid personality disorder, for example, can be impossible to treat because the affected person cannot trust and is suspicious of the therapist. Furthermore, the individual with paranoid personality does not think anything is wrong with him or her. This is a challenge for therapy because the person often drops out of therapy or refuses therapy in the first place. A person has to be motivated to change in order for therapy to be successful.

Other personality disorders are more amenable to treatment. With borderline personality disorder, for example, two therapy approaches are often quite successful. Cognitive behavioral therapy (CBT) is a treatment method that focuses on understanding and changing present behaviors, thoughts, and feelings. It is an approach that is not concerned with past traumatic experiences or figuring out the early causes of problems. Instead CBT asks what can be done now to make the person more comfortable, happier, and better functioning? The goal is to give the person problem-solving skills, realistic and positive views about self and self-worth, and more control over his or her life. For example, if the

> **WORDS IN CONTEXT**
>
> **talk therapy**
> Psychotherapy; treatment in which the individual talks over and deals with emotions, thoughts, and mental issues with a trained professional.

52

Living with Borderline Personality Disorder

At the nonprofit Mental Health Foundation in the United Kingdom, a woman identified as Kayla describes her life with BPD, hoping that other people will understand and accept. She says, in part:

> My symptoms began in early adolescence, as I quickly became aware that I was not like my peers. Separation anxiety, fear of abandonment, self-harm and emotional instability prevented me from experiencing what should have been the typical life of a teenager. I spent my days in isolation, not understanding the overwhelming emotions that attacked me from every side, often crying myself to sleep wondering why the feelings just wouldn't go away, and why I couldn't put a name to them. . . . Now in my early 30s, I feel that a new understanding of life with my diagnosis is beginning to make sense. The inability to hold down a full-time job owing to my condition has turned into the most positive career move, as I now work as a self-employed professional musician. . . . So few people are willing to look at the person behind the personality disorder. There can be such immense creativity born in the minds of those tormented by mental illness, and when harnessed through poetry, art, music or writing it can be a powerful tool for recovery. My hope is that by reading these words, that you will see the human being behind the label and perhaps that the stigma can be reduced by just one more person today.

Kayla, "Kayla's Story: Living with Borderline Personality Disorder," Mental Health Foundation, 2016. www .mentalhealth.org.uk.

person sees things in black-and-white terms—"Either I am good and perfect or I am bad and horrible"—the therapist works to help the client see that that thinking does not match reality. Together, therapist and client learn to come up with different, healthier ways for the client to think about him- or herself. If the client is having trouble with self-harm, therapist and client may work together to develop some homework to reduce and eventually eliminate the impulse. Journaling about what event precipitated the urge, what the feelings were, and how to communicate those feelings in a different way is one commonly used exercise.

Dialectical Behavior Therapy

A kind of CBT that is particularly useful for people with BPD and has been proven successful in research studies is called dialectical behavior therapy (DBT). It was developed by Linehan, who is uniquely qualified to understand the needs of people with BPD. *Dialectical* refers to opposing forces, and the seemingly opposing ideas in this therapeutic approach are acceptance and change. People learn self-acceptance while working for constructive change in behaviors and perceptions. To do this, DBT includes four main treatment arms. These include individual therapy that concentrates on motivation and encouragement; group classes with a trained teacher for learning behavior skills; telephone support, so that clients can call a coach for support during times that they need help at home; and a weekly therapy session for the therapists, teachers, and coaches, so that they will be sure they are providing the best treatment possible. DBT incorporates CBT with a technique called "mindfulness" that uses some Zen Buddhist practices and other techniques for learning to be calm, contemplative, and accepting of life in the moment. The Linehan Institute explains, "Mindfulness skills in DBT are a behavioral translation of Zen practice."[29] Linehan established the institute and developed the mindfulness approach because she personally had found such practices valuable and necessary for her own recovery. When BPD clients are very sick and suicidal, this four-pronged approach offers the greatest chance of success.

Melanie (full name withheld to protect privacy) of South Wales in the United Kingdom has BPD and describes her journey on the Linehan Institute's website. She says:

> My life was very erratic, suicide attempts and suicidal ideations [thoughts], for many years. . . . I literally went from one crisis to another. I couldn't cope with personal life, my mind was in a constant turmoil, I ruminated about the past, and catastrophised about the future; my favourite statements were "what if" and "I can't." I found it difficult to manage to hold down a job. . . .

DBT has had a dramatic impact upon my life. After the first 5 months, I finally realised that I was living again, my mind was no longer in a fog, and I could see things clearly. I no longer have suicidal ideations and I appreciate things more, I am more mindful and accepting. I radically accept things I cannot change, but change things that I can, both emotionally and literally, in my daily life.[30]

A Buddhist monk meditates in a tranquil setting. Individuals with borderline personality disorder can benefit from a combined approach of behavioral therapy and Zen Buddhist techniques for learning to be calm, contemplative, and accepting of life in the moment.

Motivated to Transform

No matter how intractable and severe a personality disorder might be, many people can get help and improve their quality of life if they truly want to change. In addition, several types of personality disorders can naturally improve as people get older. Nevertheless, personality disorders can cause lifelong misery and suffering, and psychiatrists and psychologists continue to search for the best ways to help all the people who need treatment.

CHAPTER 5

Can Personality Be Changed?

Psychologists and researchers have different opinions about whether and how much basic personality can change over a lifetime. They study how successful people can be in changing personality through choice and hard work. On the one hand, there is evidence that the fundamental personality dimensions do not change very much over time for many people. On the other hand, personality is only one part of any individual's makeup. Physical appearance and condition, intelligence, experiences, spirituality, self-identity, and independent choices all contribute to who that person is. These factors interact with personality in often unknown ways throughout an individual's lifetime. This means that even if personality remains stable, it does not have to be destiny.

Life Is Growth

Changes in personality traits have been shown to happen gradually over time for most people. Psychologist Christopher Soto has conducted several studies demonstrating that as they grow older, people become more conscientious and agreeable and less neurotic. "But these changes tend to unfold across years or decades, rather than days or weeks," Soto explains. "Sudden, dramatic changes in personality are rare."[31] People do not go from hostile to agreeable, for example, but they do move higher or lower on the continuum of some dimensions. Other researchers have identified ways that life experiences can have an effect on personality traits. For example, people who have jobs that require hardworking, responsible behaviors seem to gradually become more conscientious as they meet the demands of their job. Performing the behaviors seems to modify personality. Other studies have found that as people age, they also become less extraverted and take fewer risks and that people's level of openness decreases, as well. Research such as this demonstrates that even though personality may be 50 percent genetically determined, people are not stuck with their traits for life. Changes do happen, and often people are happier as a result.

Another way that personality traits can change—sometimes dramatically—is through therapy. In one study, psychologist Brent Roberts and his research team found that talk therapy could strongly reduce high levels of neuroticism as measured by personality testing. The team discovered that treating people for depression and anxiety (both of which are risks in very high neuroticism) resulted in significant personality changes within four to seven months. They also found that the changes lasted for years after the therapy was completed (suggesting they were real personality changes). The researchers also found increased extraversion scores in these people; they became more sociable and more responsive to positive emotions.

Just Wanting to Change

In another study, Roberts and his colleague Nathan W. Hudson found that most people wish they could change some part of their personality. Many want to become more emotionally stable; others wish to be more conscientious (hardworking, organized, and goal oriented); and some wish they were more extraverted, open, or agreeable. Roberts and Hudson say that no scientific proof exists that such changes are possible, but there are plenty of anecdotes or stories from individuals that such change is possible.

When Brandon Green was twenty-nine years old, for example, he decided that he did not like his personality. He realized that he was an unhappy person. He felt negative about the world and was often angry or jealous of others. He was so intro-verted that he stayed by himself much of the time. Green made a conscious decision to try to change his ways. He saw a cog-nitive behavioral therapist for eighteen months and also kept a journal and read books about changing one's perspectives. He worked at analyzing himself and his thoughts, practiced being calm in stressful situations, and pushed himself to understand

Human personalities are complex. Two people might have the same extraversion score on a personality test, but one of these individuals might love mountain climbing and thrill seeking, while the other might be very social but not interested in high-risk activities.

Damaging to the Personality

Sometimes brain injury can affect the personality, such as after a stroke, an accident, or anytime the brain is deprived of oxygen for a long period. It all depends on the part of the brain that has been damaged. For example, damage to the frontal lobes or the amygdala can cause a change in emotional control, an inability to inhibit expressing thoughts and feelings; impulsiveness; and an increase in hostile, angry emotions. Brain injury also can cause increased depression, anxiety, and other psychological issues. Some people with brain injuries can lose their empathy for others or lose their energy and motivations and become apathetic. Others who were quiet people may become talkative and entertaining. The personality changes can be temporary; modifiable with time, medication, and therapy; or permanent. Coping with personality change is hard for the individual affected and for family members. James Cracknell suffered a severe brain injury in 2010 when he was cycling and was hit by a truck. He and his family are still adjusting to his personality changes. He says, "Some avenues are shut off to me now but I'm determined to open new ones."

Quoted in Elizabeth Grice, "James Cracknell: Hopefully We'll Get Back to Where We Once Were," *Telegraph* (London), October 19, 2012. www.telegraph.co.uk.

why he experienced stress so often. He also took up a hobby—photography—that got him out of his apartment and into social situations where he had to talk to people. Green explains about his efforts, "If you are more negative, you have a feeling that bad stuff can happen at every turn. You have to question if that is just coming from you because you are living through a sour lens." Today Green feels that his efforts, while a lot of hard work, have paid off. He is still introverted but not withdrawn from the world. He learned to change his negative expectations into more positive ones. He likes himself, enjoys social situations, and makes friends. He even thinks his introversion helped him change. He says, "Being introspective and attempting to be honest with myself and others has helped me greatly in becoming a happier, more outgoing person."[32]

Many researchers question whether people such as Brandon Green are really changing their personalities or just modifying their behavior to resist and overcome their basic tendencies and personalities. They are not sure that a person's basic nature can be dramatically altered. Nevertheless, almost all experts agree that people can change how they deal with their personality traits and change behavior and reactions so that they are happier and more satisfied with their lives. This is because basic traits are not all there is to human beings.

Personality Is More than Traits

Dan P. McAdams is a psychologist and personality expert who has developed a theory that explains how individual human beings become their unique selves. He says that personality is more complex than the five basic factors measured by personality tests. Personality is made up of three layers, or levels. The first level is composed of the big five personality traits. They are determined genetically and by early childhood experiences. The second level is the characteristic behavior patterns that grow out of the big five traits, but these patterns are different for everyone. They describe the individual's personal concerns. McAdams explains, "They speak to what people want, often during particular periods in their lives or within particular domains of action, and what life methods people use (strategies, plans, defenses, and so on) to get what they want or avoid getting what they do not want over time, in particular places, and/or with respect to particular roles."[33] In short, this second level represents each person's values and goals. As an example, two people could take a personality test and both score exactly the same on the extraversion dimension. Yet these two people would have different wants and, thus, different experiences. One person might love mountain climbing, thrill seeking, and taking physical risks, while the other might not be at all enthusiastic about risky endeavors but might still be highly social, involved with people, a partygoer, and a successful salesperson. There are many different behaviors through which extraversion can be expressed. These behaviors are choices that each individual makes, and they are choices and behaviors that are under each person's control.

The third level described by McAdams is the personal life story. Everyone has a personal life story that goes on inside their heads. The stories are what people tell themselves to define who they are and explain to themselves why they are the way they are. Everyone's personal story is unique. McAdams calls this story each person's identity and explains that it is the "evolving *story* of the self—an ongoing narrative that reconstructs the past and imagines the future in order to provide a person's life with a sense of unity and purpose."[34]

Most people begin developing their own life stories when they are teenagers. The stories describe how different events were meaningful to them or how they learned from them. For example, a young man might tell his story of making the football team after much practice and struggle and then say he learned from this experience that hard work pays off. He might then go on to predict that he will be successful in college because he knows how to fight for what he wants. A high school girl might remember the time in childhood when her best friend suffered a terrible, prolonged illness and believe that the experience explains why she wants to become a physician someday.

Older people have different ways of telling their life stories, too. Two people with extremely similar personality profiles, for instance, might have had similar career experiences. Neither may have been very successful at climbing the corporate ladder or making lots of money. But one might tell her story as one of failure and disappointment, while the other tells his as how lucky he was to avoid getting caught up in material success and to learn to experience the beauty of nature and family.

Good Stories

Those adults who are the most productive, emotionally healthy, caring, and happiest individuals seem to tell stories with similar themes. They are generally positive stories. These are told by people who feel a purpose in life and believe that they are making a positive impact on others and the world. McAdams calls these people generative because they are trying to generate, produce, and create in a way that will help their society and future generations. He says generative adults usually tell stories like this (with varying specific details):

> I learned in childhood that I have a special gift. At the same time, I see (and am moved by) suffering and injustice in my world. As a result, I come to believe that my personal destiny is to have some positive impact on others. In adolescence I internalize a belief system that sustains my commitment to improving the world. I will never abandon these core beliefs. Over the course of my adult life, I struggle to reconcile my strong needs for power and independence with my equally strong needs for love and community. Bad things happen to me, but good outcomes often follow. My suffering is usually redeemed, as I continue to progress, to learn, to improve. Looking to the future, I expect the things I have generated will continue to grow and flourish, even in a dangerous world.[35]

Changing Goals and Values

How can people develop positive personal stories like this? Even if personality traits do not change much over time, goals, values, and personal stories can and do change. Much depends on each individual's motivation and how he or she decides to interpret life events. Even how people cope with their personality traits is often under conscious control. Sometimes, change can be relatively easy. For example, a woman high in extraversion may enjoy regular mountain climbing. Then, when she becomes a mother, she may decide to give up the pursuit for the sake of her child. She does not want to take unnecessary risks because she places more value on being sure she does not leave her child motherless due

Individuals can control—and even change—their own personality traits. Alcoholics who want to stop drinking might know that they have poor impulse control. So rather than trying to limit how much they drink, they choose to completely give up alcohol.

to an accident. Daniel Nettle offers another example—alcoholics whose goal is to stop drinking. Such people have poor impulse control (low conscientiousness), so they consciously decide not to try limiting themselves to drinking a couple of cocktails twice a week. They have to give up alcohol completely. Nettle explains, "They know that if they start, their personality will not allow them to stop, and so they do not put themselves in the position of having started."[36] This kind of control is much harder than giving up a hobby, but many alcoholics use their values and goals (McAdams's second level) to accomplish it.

Psychologist Brian Little made a conscious decision to override the strong introversion that was part of his personality. He changed his patterns of behavior by acting the part of what he wanted to be. As a professor in the classroom, Little did not want to be quiet and introverted. He wanted to interest and engage his students. So he learned to pretend to be extraverted. He explains:

> I'm off the bottom of the scale as an introvert. But because of something that matters dearly to me—which is the personal project of professing with passion and alliterating in a public place—I will act as an extrovert when I'm lecturing. I'll speak loudly as you do when you're addressing a class at the beginning. I'll gesticulate wildly. I hope not too wildly because I think we need not to be overbearing when we're professing—but we need to keep students awake at eight in the morning.[37]

Little's students are surprised when he tells them he is introverted because he is so entertaining in the classroom. He thinks he is a good example for them—and everyone—that personality traits do not have to dictate how people react to the world.

Changing Personal Stories

Learning to tell a new personal story (personality's third level) can control and even modify personality traits, although it takes determination and hard work. Narrative therapy is one method used by psychologists and therapists to help people learn to tell different, more positive stories about themselves. Together, therapist and client examine stories that are negative, such as "I am a hopeless person" or "I am a juvenile offender and a thief" or "I fail at whatever I try to do." Then the therapist helps redefine experiences, thoughts, and emotions in a more positive way. It is a process that takes time. People might be asked to remember a time when they did something good, acted with determination,

WORDS IN CONTEXT

generative
In psychology, productive, socially responsible, and capable of caring for others.

or overcame a problem. They are helped to see that the story they tell themselves is only a problem, not a true representation of their entire life. Perhaps the client is a person who once got into trouble with the law for stealing but never did anything like that again. This person also happens to be a good, supportive friend to others. This person can tell him- or herself a more accurate or alternative story that not only redefines past behavior but also enhances belief in his or her positive characteristics. The person can decide to learn from past problems, expect positive outcomes, and have a bright future. McAdams and his colleague Lisa Janis say of learning alternative stories, "A good story solves problems and broadens a person's life."[38] And such

Pretending to Be Different

Personality researcher Brian Little says that many people can adopt free traits, which are basically pretend traits that individuals use to meet a major goal in their lives. Little acts like an extravert in the classroom because he wants to interest his students. Other people, he says, can pretend to be conscientious at work instead of the lazy, careless people that they are comfortable being at home. Extraverted people can act like introverts at work and spend long, quiet hours alone to be productive at their jobs. People can fake such personality traits quite successfully when they think they need to. Little's research student Sanna Balsari-Palsule wanted to know how difficult it is for people to go against their natural personalities and pretend to be different. She studied the use of free traits with three hundred individuals in a workplace in the United Kingdom. She has found that pretending to be different can cause stress and emotional exhaustion. It is especially hard for extraverts to pretend to be introverted. Both Little and Balsari-Palsule recommend that people take time during each day or on the weekend to restore themselves and give in to their true natures. Extraverts, for example, need to socialize, and people with low conscientiousness need to take weekends off with no plans and no expectations to meet. People can stand to act against their basic personalities, but only for a limited amount of time.

stories really change how a person expresses personality traits and how happy he or she is with life.

Many people high in neuroticism have trouble telling positive stories about themselves. Bad things may happen in their lives, and good things often do not get woven into their stories. For example, some people see themselves as failures because they always got average grades in school instead of excellent ones. Perhaps when their school years ended they got average jobs and never advanced in their careers. They see themselves as never doing anything outstanding and therefore of little worth. Reframing that story might help such people see their lives in a different way. Maybe they decided not to waste their lives seeking money and status. Instead, they chose other avenues in which to focus energy and purpose. They have many friends and loving families who admire them. They volunteer to help the homeless and coach a children's sports team. They have succeeded in what matters most to them after all. Seeing the truth of the positive story helps people let go of negative emotions and makes life fulfilling.

Bigger than Our Traits

No one has to accept life or his or her personality as it is. Everyone can use self-knowledge to make different choices, and everyone has the freedom to adjust and adapt to their personalities and use those traits to build the life that they want and value. Nettle calls it "Singing With Your Own Voice,"[39] and that is what he urges everyone to do.

SOURCE NOTES

Introduction: What Is Personality?

1. American Psychological Association, "Personality," 2016. www.apa.org.

2. Robert R. McCrae and Paul T. Costa Jr., "Chapter 5: The Five-Factor Theory of Personality," in *Handbook of Personality: Theory and Research*, 3rd ed., eds. Oliver P. John, Richard W. Robins, and Lawrence A. Pervin. New York: Guilford, 2008, p. 159.

Chapter 1: How Does Personality Develop?

3. Benjamin Spock and Robert Needlman, *Dr. Spock's Baby and Child Care*, 9th ed. New York: Gallery, 2012, p. 651.

4. Child Development Institute, "The 9 Temperament Traits." https://childdevelopmentinfo.com.

5. Quoted in Lisa Trei, "Happy Faces Trigger Different Brain Reactions in Extroverts and Introverts," *Stanford Report*, July 10, 2002. http://news.stanford.edu.

6. Quoted in Nick Collins, "It's Nature, Not Nurture: Personality Lies in Genes, Twin Study Shows," *Telegraph* (London), May 16, 2012. www.telegraph.co.uk.

7. Quoted in Tanya Lewis, "Twins Separated at Birth Reveal Staggering Influence of Genetics," LiveScience, August 11, 2014. www.livescience.com.

8. Robert Needlman, "Temperament: What Is It?," Raising Children Network, March 2006. http://raisingchildren.net.au.

9. Quoted in LiveScience staff, "Personality Set for Life by 1st Grade, Study Suggests," LiveScience, August 6, 2010. www.livescience.com.

Chapter 2: What Are Different Personality Styles and Traits?

10. Quoted in Daniel Nettle, *Personality: What Makes You the Way You Are.* New York: Oxford University Press, 2007, p. 88.

11. Nettle, *Personality*, p. 101.

12. Susan Cain, "Must Great Leaders Be Gregarious?," *New York Times*, September 15, 2012. www.nytimes.com.

13. Nettle, *Personality*, p. 111.

14. Quoted in Nettle, *Personality*, p. 170.

15. Art Markman, "Are Successful People Nice?," *Harvard Business Review*, February 9, 2012. https://hbr.org.

Chapter 3: What Can Be Learned from Personality Tests?

16. OutOfService, "The Big Five Project: Personality Test," 2015. www.outofservice.com.

17. Quoted in Amanda L. Chan, "Why Being Neurotic Could Actually Be a Good Thing," *Huffington Post*, April 9, 2014. www.huffingtonpost.com.

18. Quoted in Stacy Notaras Murphy, "Getting to Know You," *Counseling Today*, February 25, 2014. http://ct.counseling.org.

19. Quoted in Keith Wagstaff, "Why Do You Love Personality Quizzes? Experts Break It Down," NBC News, August 4, 2014. www.nbcnews.com.

20. Samuel D. Gosling, Peter J. Rentfrow, and William B. Swann Jr., "A Very Brief Measure of the Big-Five Personality Domains," *Journal of Research in Personality*, 2003, p. 523. http://citeseerx.ist.psu.edu.

21. Robert R. McCrae and Paul T. Costa Jr., "The Stability of Personality: Observations and Evaluations," *Current Directions in Psychological Science*, December 1994. http://cdp.sagepub.com.

22. Nettle, *Personality*, p. 45.

23. Nettle, *Personality*, p. 43.

Chapter 4: What Are Personality Disorders?

24. American Psychiatric Association, "What Are Personality Disorders?," 2016. www.psychiatry.org.

25. Quoted in Benedict Carey, "Expert on Mental Illness Reveals Her Own Fight," *New York Times*, June 23, 2011. www.nytimes.com.

26. Quoted in Scott O. Lilienfeld and Hal Arkowitz, "Diagnosis of Borderline Personality Disorder Is Often Flawed," *Scientific American*, January 1, 2012. www.scientificamerican.com.

27. Fred K. Berger, "Obsessive-Compulsive Personality Disorder," MedlinePlus, October 31, 2014. https://medlineplus.gov.

28. Avoidant Personality Disorder, home page. http://avoidant personality.com.

29. Linehan Institute: Behavioral Tech, "What Is DBT?" http://be havioraltech.org.

30. Quoted in Linehan Institute, "DBT Stories," 2016. www.line haninstitute.org.

Chapter 5: Can Personality Be Changed?

31. Christopher Soto, "Personality Can Change Over a Lifetime, and Usually for the Better," NPR, June 30, 2016. www.npr.org.

32. Quoted in Elizabeth Bernstein, "Personality Research Says Change in Major Traits Occurs Naturally," *Wall Street Journal,* April 22, 2014. www.wsj.com.

33. Quoted in John D. Mayer, "Three Levels of Knowing a Person," *The Personality Analyst* (blog), *Psychology Today*, November 8, 2010. www.psychologytoday.com.

34. Quoted in Joshua Wilt, "An Interview with 2012 Jack Block Award Winner Dan McAdams," *P*, October, 2013. www.personality-arp.org.

35. Dan P. McAdams, *The Redemptive Self: Stories Americans Live By.* New York: Oxford University Press, 2006, p. 10.

36. Nettle, *Personality*, p. 240.

37. Brian Little, podcast interview with Adam Grant, "Author Brian Little on Personality and the 'Art of Well-Being,'" Wharton School, University of Pennsylvania, April 27, 2015. http://knowledge.wharton.upenn.edu.

38. Dan P. McAdams and Lisa Janis, "Narrative Identity and Narrative Therapy," in *The Handbook of Narrative and Psychotherapy: Practice, Theory, and Research*, eds. Lynne E. Angus and John McLeod. Thousand Oaks, CA: Sage, 2004, p. 169.

39. Nettle, *Personality*, p. 234.

FOR FURTHER RESEARCH

Books

Susan Cain et al., *Quiet Power: The Secret Strengths of Introverts.* New York: Dial, 2016.

Bernardo J. Carducci and Lisa Kaiser, *Shyness: The Ultimate Teen Guide.* New York: Rowman and Littlefield, 2015.

Michelle Harris and Julie Beer, *This or That? 4: Even More Wacky Choices to Reveal the Hidden You.* Washington, DC: National Geographic Kids, 2016.

Mary C. Lamia, *Understanding Myself: A Kid's Guide to Intense Emotions and Strong Feelings.* Washington, DC: Magination, 2011.

Wendy L. Moss, *Bounce Back: How to Be a Resilient Kid*. Washington, DC: Magination, 2015.

Jacqueline B. Toner and Claire A.B. Freeland, *Depression: A Teen's Guide to Survive and Thrive*. Washington, DC: Magination, 2016.

Marcus Weeks, *Heads Up Psychology.* New York: DK, 2014.

Internet Sources

National Geographic Kids, "Personality Quizzes," 2016. http://kids.nationalgeographic.com/explore/adventure_pass/personality-quizzes.

Chris Wilson, "America's Mood Map: An Interactive Guide to the United States of Attitude," *Time*, October 22, 2013. http://time.com/7612/americas-mood-map-an-interactive-guide-to-the-united-states-of-attitude.

Websites

Big Five Project: Personality Test (www.outofservice.com/bigfive). For people aged thirteen or older, this site offers a five-factor personality test and uses the answers for research studies. A free personality profile is available for educational purposes.

Linehan Institute (www.linehaninstitute.org). This is the official website of the Linehan Institute, founded by Marsha M. Linehan; it explains DBT for people with BPD and other complex disorders. Click on the "Resources" link to see videos about the therapy and learning the skills for teens and young adults. Click "Contact Us" to find out how to locate a therapist.

Personality Tests (www.outofservice.com). Just for fun, people can access several tests here to find out what their musical tastes say about them, what *Star Wars* character is most like them, and more. Jeff Potter, the site's founder, has worked with several university researchers over the years to help them gather data from Internet users on the site.

INDEX

cognitive behavioral therapy (CBT), 52–53

comedians, 29

conscientiousness, 25–27

    definition of, 8

continuum, definition of, 8

correlation, definition of, 17

cortex, definition of, 27

Costa, Paul T., Jr., 6–7, 42

Cracknell, James, 60

creativity

    mental disorders and, 53

    openness and, 8, 32

depression, 28, 29

DeYoung, Colin, 27

dialectical behavior therapy (DBT), 54–55

distractibility trait, 10–11

dopamine, 25

Dostoevsky, Fyodor, 29

drug addiction, 27

Dugatkin, Lee, 14

emotions, 5, 15

    brain injuries and, 60

    in cluster B personality disorders, 48

    intensity trait and, 11

    prefrontal cortex and, 27

response to

    in extroverts, 23

    in introverts, 24

empathy, 29–30, 48, 60

environment

    prenatal, 20

    role in personality development, 18–20

Essig, Todd, 38

extraversion, 22–25

    definition of, 8

free traits, 66

Freud, Sigmund, 6, **7**

gambling problems, 27

Gates, Bill, 25, **26**

generative, definition of, 65

gene(s)

    definition of, 12

    mutations/variants in, 12–13

    temperament and, 14–15

Goldberg, Lewis, 6–7

Gosling, Samuel D., 14, 36, 40

Green, Brandon, 58–59

Greengross, Gil, 29

group therapy, 37

openness, 31–33
  definition of, 8

paranoid personality
  disorder, 46–48
  treatment of, 52
parenting styles, 18–19
persistence trait, 11
personality
  age of stabilization of, 10,
    21, 42
  in animals, 14
  definition of, 5
  effects of life experiences
    on, 57–58
  environmental role in,
    18–20
  five-factor model of, 6–8
  genetic *vs.* environmental
    determination of, 10
  levels of, 61–62
  and long-term space
    travel, 32
  reasons for defining, 9
  theories of, 6–7
  See also trait(s)
personality disorders
  cluster A, 46–48
  cluster B, 48–50
  cluster C, 50–51
  prevalence of, 28–29, 45

treatment of, 51–53
  See also therapies
personality tests/testing,
  34–35, 39
  limitations of, 43–44
  reasons for, 35–38
  reliability/validity of, 39–41
personal life stories, 62–63
  alternative, learning, 65–67
  definition of, 62
phobias, 28
post-traumatic stress, 28
Prinstein, Mitch, 38
profile(s), personality
  definition of, 35
  stability of, 41–42
prosocial behavior, 30
  definition of 4, 33

regularity trait, 11
reliability
  definition of, 39
  of personality tests, 39–40
risk taking, 23–24, 27, 58
Roberts, Brent, 58

Segal, Nancy, 17–18
self-harm, definition of, 49
self-report, definition of, 42
sensory threshold trait, 11

PICTURE CREDITS

Cover: Shutterstock.com/Lakov Filimonov

4: Maury Aaseng

7: akg-images

13: iStockphoto/PeopleImages

16: Thinkstock Images/iStock

19: Depositphotos/sylv1rob1

24: Depositphotos/mihtiander

26: Shutterstock.com/JStone

31: Depositphotos/monkeybusiness

36: iStockphoto/Alvarez

41: iStockphoto.com

47: Shutterstock.com/Artsplav

55: Shutterstock/Alohaflaminggo

59: Thinkstock Images/iStock

64: Shutterstock.com/Marcos Mesa Sam Wordley

ABOUT THE AUTHOR

Toney Allman holds a BS in psychology from Ohio State University and an MA in clinical psychology from the University of Hawaii. She currently lives in Virginia, where she enjoys a rural lifestyle and researching and writing about a variety of topics for students.